The Be-Attitudes

Attitudes that "Ought to Be"

By
Pastor Bill Jenkins

Table of Contents

Introduction

Jesus prepared privately for 30 years before being led into the wilderness to be tested three times by the devil. He fasted for 40 days and 40 nights and overcame every temptation the enemy threw His way. In Luke 4:14, Jesus came out of the wilderness in the power of the Holy Spirit. Jesus did not preach one sermon, perform one miracle, or heal one person until He learned how to overcome all the tricks, traps, and temptations of the enemy. When Jesus came out of the wilderness, He immediately went home to Nazareth and went to church on the Sabbath. Someone handed him the Old Testament book of Isaiah, and He stood up and read Isaiah 61:1-2a,
"The Spirit of the Lord God is upon me; because the Lord hath anointed me to preach good tidings unto the meek; he hath sent me to bind up the brokenhearted, to proclaim liberty to the captives, and the opening of the prison to them that are bound; To proclaim the acceptable year of the Lord,"

This is how Jesus began his ministry that only lasted around three years. After reading those scriptures from Isaiah, Jesus began to draw attention from others, and crowds started to follow. Jesus recruited disciples, and they became part of the first school of the Holy Spirit. Jesus traveled throughout Israel preaching in synagogues and in the streets the need for people to repent. Jesus also healed the sick and delivered people possessed by the devil. As the crowds began to grow, Jesus went up to the mountain and gave His first public sermon. In this sermon, Jesus addressed several topics in over 106 verses found in Matthew 5-7. Jesus mentioned subjects such as…

- The importance of being salt and light in an ungodly world.
- The importance of the Old Testament to not be destroyed but to have it fulfilled.
- The importance of not being angry and not speaking evil about others.
- The importance of forgiveness.
- The importance of faithfulness and loyalty in marriage.
- The importance of keeping your promises.
- The importance of loving your enemies.
- The importance of giving to the needy.
- The importance of combining prayer and fasting.
- The importance of being totally sold out to Christ.
- The importance of not judging others.
- The importance of fulfilling the Golden Rule.
- The importance of staying on the straight and narrow pathway of God.
- The importance of bearing fruit.

- The importance of building your foundation on the solid rock of Christ.

All of these subjects are necessary and important. However, Jesus starts His very first sermon by talking about... ATTITUDES. Jesus understood what all of us need to understand and that is, "Your attitude determines your altitude."

Bad attitude = Low altitude
Godly attitude = High altitude

Learning to have a godly attitude in an ungodly world is really what this book is all about. Jesus gives us eight godly attitudes that will guarantee the blessing of God upon our lives. Throughout scripture, we learn that every promise has a condition. If you meet the condition, then you will receive the promise. It is really simple!! Blessings always come to the obedient.

"And it shall come to pass, if thou shalt hearken diligently unto the voice of the Lord thy God, to observe and to do all his commandments which I command thee this day, that the Lord thy God will set thee on high above all nations of the earth: And all these blessings shall come on thee, and overtake thee, if thou shalt hearken unto the voice of the Lord thy God." Deuteronomy 28:1-2

It has never been as important as it is today to have a godly attitude and a scriptural perspective concerning this life. These ten verses in Matthew 5:3-12 release eight attitudes that will change your life and set you up for success.

> *"3 Blessed are the poor in spirit: for theirs is the kingdom of heaven.*
> *4 Blessed are they that mourn: for they shall be comforted.*
> *5 Blessed are the meek: for they shall inherit the earth.*
> *6 Blessed are they which do hunger and thirst after righteousness: for they shall be filled.*
> *7 Blessed are the merciful: for they shall obtain mercy.*
> *8 Blessed are the pure in heart: for they shall see God.*
> *9 Blessed are the peacemakers: for they shall be called the children of God.*
> *10 Blessed are they which are persecuted for righteousness' sake: for theirs is the kingdom of heaven.*
> *11 Blessed are ye, when men shall revile you, and persecute you, and shall say all manner of evil against you falsely, for my sake.*
> *12 Rejoice, and be exceeding glad: for great is your reward in heaven: for so persecuted they the prophets which were before you."*

As we take an in-depth look at each of these eight attitudes, allow the Lord to open up your heart to truly search your heart for areas that need to change. God wants to bless you above and beyond what you can dream or imagine, but He needs your cooperation. If it is important to God for us to have a godly attitude, then it needs to be important to us to have good and godly attitudes. Let us dig into God's Word and allow the Lord to give us an attitude adjustment.

Chapter 1
WHAT IS A BE-ATTITUDE?

Simply put, a Be-attitude is an attitude that "ought to be" in our lives to insure the blessing of God. An attitude is a feeling or emotion that gets established in your mind that affects your behavior. As Christians, it is important to root out all ungodly mindsets and only display our natural emotions in a way that pleases God. The Beatitudes are a road map from God to guide us into victory. When Jesus gave His sermon on the Mount, the first subject in His first message was on attitudes. So, your attitude is extremely important to establishing success in your life. The eight Beatitudes are sort of Jesus' New Testament version of the Ten Commandments that God gave to Moses in the Old Testament. The Beatitudes signaled a shift from the external approach of the outward righteousness of the Pharisees, to an inward examination of our heart. All of the Pharisee's teachings focused on outward righteousness and now Jesus is altering that wrong pharisaical philosophy to focus in on inward righteousness. Jesus was teaching us that our outward conduct flows out of inward character. In other words, whatever is on the inside, will ultimately manifest on the outside.

"But the Lord said unto Samuel, Look not on his countenance, or on the height of his stature; because

I have refused him: for the Lord seeth not as man seeth; for man looketh on the outward appearance, but the Lord looketh on the heart." 1 Samuel 16:7

If our inward roots are good, then our outward fruits will be good. If our inward hearts are right before God, then our actions will follow outwardly and externally. Jesus gave us eight attitudes that ought to be in our lives if we want to be blessed. Being blessed is about enjoying life instead of enduring life. These attitudes help us to establish the Christian character that is necessary to please God.

These attitudes from Jesus also help us to avoid becoming like the Pharisees in our approach to others. Jesus hated the ideology and attitudes of the Pharisees.

Bad Attitudes of the Pharisees

- The Pharisees were motivated by attention from man.

    "But all their works they do for to be seen of men: they make broad their phylacteries, and enlarge the borders of their garments, And love the uppermost rooms at feasts, and the chief seats in the synagogues, And greetings in the markets, and to be called of men, Rabbi, Rabbi." Matthew 23:5-7

The Beatitudes put the attention upon God, not upon man.

- The Pharisees made it hard to enter the Kingdom of God.

"But woe unto you, scribes and Pharisees, hypocrites! for ye shut up the kingdom of heaven against men: for ye neither go in yourselves, neither suffer ye them that are entering to go in." Matthew 23:13

The Beatitudes help us to understand our need to depend on God for everything and never be independent.

- The Pharisees focused on outward works.

"Woe unto you, scribes and Pharisees, hypocrites! for ye make clean the outside of the cup and of the platter, but within they are full of extortion and excess. Thou blind Pharisee, cleanse first that which is within the cup and platter, that the outside of them may be clean also." Matthew 23:25-26

Beatitudes cause us to focus on inward character and developing the fruit of the Spirit.

- The Pharisees focused on judgment.

  "Woe unto you, scribes and Pharisees, hypocrites! for ye pay tithe of mint and anise and cumin, and have omitted the weightier matters of the law, judgment, mercy, and faith: these ought ye to have done, and not to leave the other undone. Ye blind guides, which strain at a gnat, and swallow a camel." Matthew 23:23-24

  Beatitudes focus on mercy and grace.

- The Pharisees were unwilling to do what they required others to do.

  "For they bind heavy burdens and grievous to be borne, and lay them on men's shoulders; but they themselves will not move them with one of their fingers." Matthew 23:4

  Beatitudes teach us to focus on what we do for others; instead of what others do to us.

The word beatitude is not a word that is even mentioned in the Bible, but it is a word that has the potential to produce blessings as you put these attitudes that ought to be in practice in your daily life.

Chapter 2
BLESSED ARE THE POOR IN SPIRIT…

The phrase "poor in spirit" is definitely an interesting statement. Being "poor in spirit" is about being humble. In the Greek, "poor in spirit" refers to someone who is meager or lacking an adequate supply of something. The attitude that God wants us to have is one of dependence on God regardless of how blessed we may already be. It is never good to be autonomous and do things independent of God. Outside of the Lord, we are nothing and can do nothing. Without God we are morally and spiritually bankrupt.

Seven Characteristics of People Who are Poor in Spirit

1. They are not too proud to ask for help.

   Proud people are self-reliant and figure everything out on their own. They are great helpers but not so good at asking for help. They have created an unhealthy balance between being helped and helping others. Asking for help does not make you weak, it makes you wise.

2. They are not trying to impress God; they are trying to please God.

You do not impress the officials of NASA with a paper airplane any more than you can impress the creator of the universe with your human efforts. You should always attempt to please God but never try to impress God.

3. They live day to day.

We all know what it means to be poor. A poor person lives day by day and does not have an abundance of possessions saved up for the future. Each day, a poor person needs to earn or receive the things they need to survive for that day. Their life and work are concerned with necessities: food, clothing, and shelter. They do not have time or money for vacations and pleasant diversions. Someone poor in spirit is someone who lives in their spiritual life the way those who are poor in body live their physical lives. The physically poor person works each day to receive their bread. The spiritually poor person prays each day to receive spiritual nourishment from the Lord: "Give us this day our daily bread."

4. They never get unnecessarily distracted.

The physically poor person does not have time for unnecessary distractions. They focus on the majors of life and not the minors. The spiritually poor person sees that they must always tend to the necessities of their spiritual life: prayer, the Word of God, and obedience. They do not give in to distractions.

5. They know their severe need for Christ.

   A person who is poor in spirit realizes that they are nothing, have nothing, and can do nothing without God. As Jesus said in John 15:5, *"Without Me, you can do nothing."* Our sin puts us all in a helpless, hopeless, and desperate state. Outside of Christ, we are spiritually and morally bankrupt.

6. They do not become defensive when held accountable.

   They are passive and listen. They do not get aggressive and defensive. The person who is poor in spirit is the person who has been silenced by God and seeks only to speak what they have learned from God. Too many people want the last word in a conversation. People who are poor in spirit give others the last word.

7. They never think or believe they are better than anyone.

Pride is one of the seven deadly sins, and it will definitely destroy you. We need to avoid being prideful in all areas of our lives such as:

- Racial pride
- Spiritual pride
- Class pride

All pride is bad!! In many ways, being poor in spirit is about walking, talking, and living in humility. All our actions should be done in a modest manner, never drawing attention to ourselves. Our purpose should be for us to decrease and for God to increase. Humble people do not just think less of themselves, but they think of themselves less. They put others above themselves. They are never dismissive of others, but they show respect towards everyone they come across. Being poor in spirit releases a great promise into the lives of those who walk in humility. Matthew 5:3 says, when we obey God's command to be poor in spirit, then the kingdom of Heaven is ours. That is a big blessing!!

- Heaven is ours!
- Healing is ours!
- Deliverance is ours!
- Salvation is ours!
- Joy is ours!
- Peace is ours!
- Hope is ours!

THE KINGDOM OF HEAVEN IS OURS!!!

The book of Matthew is the only book in the Bible that mentions the specific phrase "kingdom of Heaven." Matthew mentions the phrase over 30 times in his 28 chapters. The "kingdom of Heaven" refers to Jesus establishing the principles, the peace, and the power of Heaven on the earth. Whatever is in Heaven is possible right now on Earth as Jesus rules as king over our worldly kingdom. Everything the Kingdom of God offers is ours when we walk in obedience to God. Humility is not easy, but it is possible the closer we draw ourselves to the Lord. Start asking God to help you walk in humility and demonstrate the characteristics of being poor in spirit, so you can experience all the blessings God has for you in this life.

...FOR THEIRS IS THE KINGDOM
OF HEAVEN.

SUMMARY

Beatitude:

Poor in Spirit

Opposing Attitude:

Pride

God's Reward:

Kingdom of Heaven

How to Develop this Attitude:

"Submit yourselves therefore to God. Resist the devil, and he will flee from you.[8] Draw nigh to God, and he will draw nigh to you. Cleanse your hands, ye sinners; and purify your hearts, ye double minded.[9] Be afflicted, and mourn, and weep: let your laughter be turned to mourning, and your joy to heaviness.[10] Humble yourselves in the sight of the Lord, and he shall lift you up." James 4:7-10

Chapter 3
BLESSED ARE THEY WHO MOURN…

If you have suffered a loss or experienced a tragedy, God wants to give you permission to mourn. You do not have to suck it up, hold it in, or tie a knot and survive. It is okay to grieve. It is okay to cry; your tears are liquid prayers and God reads the words on every tear from your eyes. It is okay to grieve and mourn…God cares!!

Six Facts Concerning Grief

1. Grief is normal.

   Grief is not a disease. It is a normal, human response to a significant loss in your life. People may encourage you to "be strong" or "not to cry", but how sad it would be if someone you cared about died and you did not cry or acted as if nothing had happened. I would like to think that someone will miss me enough to shed a tear after I am gone. When you lose someone special from your life, you are going to grieve. Your grief is saying that you miss the person and that you are struggling to adjust to a life without that relationship.

2. Grief is unpredictable.

    You may experience a wide variety of feelings and emotions when you are grieving. Sadness, crying, shock, panic, depression, guilt, and anger are associated with grief. Grief is unpredictable. You cannot present it in a neat, predictable, pretty package.

3. Grief is personal.

    Do not let other people tell you how to grieve. Everyone experiences loss in a different way. Your loss seems like the worst possible thing that could have happened to you. Other people who want to share their experiences with you are just that, "their experiences." People may sincerely try and help, but your pain is your pain. It may take longer than others are comfortable with because pain is personal.

4. Grief is life changing.

    Grief will change you, so do not expect to be your old self again. When a person experiences a true loss, they have to learn to live without someone who has meant a lot to them, and I promise you, that alone will change you.

5. Grief is about loss.

Grief is what we experience after we lose someone or something significant in our lives. Death, divorce, loss of a pet, breaking of a friendship, betrayal, or even the loss of a job can all cause grief.

6. Grief is impartial.

Grief does not care who you are, it affects us all. Everyone deals with grief. It is not biased or prejudice. Unfortunately, every age, every color, every gender, and every nationality around the world is acquainted with grief. To not have pain is not human.

In Matthew 5:4, Jesus gives us permission to have an attitude of mourning when we are legitimately suffering a loss in our lives. Jesus also reassures us that we will be comforted in the middle of our pain. True comfort releases strength, encouragement, and relief from pain. That is exactly what God wants to give us when we are dealing with a great loss in our lives. The comfort God offers will ease our pain and bring strength to our troubled souls.

Pain is unpleasant and creates discomfort. Pain is a burden that causes agony. It is impossible to turn on the television without seeing a commercial or advertisement for some pain killer or pain reducer that can help ease the pain. God does not want you to self-medicate or find a way to deal with the pain that life can bring. God wants you to turn to Him and allow Jesus to be the solution to your mourning.

"How God anointed Jesus of Nazareth with the Holy Ghost and with power: who went about doing good, and healing all that were oppressed of the devil; for God was with him." Acts 10:38

"The Lord is nigh unto them that are of a broken heart; and saveth such as be of a contrite spirit." Psalm 34:18

Jesus also does not want us to waste our pain because pain has a purpose. Your pain has a purpose!!

The Purpose of Pain

1. Pain forces us to <u>look</u> towards God.

    Pain causes us to acknowledge our need for help. Pain compels us to realize we are not in control. Pain makes us depend on someone other than ourselves.

"Look unto me, and be ye saved, all the ends of the earth: for I am God, and there is none else." Isaiah 45:22

2. Pain forces us to <u>lean</u> on God.

    "Come unto me, all ye that labour and are heavy laden, and I will give you rest." Matthew 11:28

3. Pain forces us to <u>learn</u> from God.

    "And though the Lord give you the bread of adversity, and the water of affliction, yet shall not thy teachers be removed into a corner any more, but thine eyes shall see thy teachers:" Isaiah 30:20

4. Pain forces us to <u>long</u> for God.

    "My soul longeth, yea, even fainteth for the courts of the Lord: my heart and my flesh crieth out for the living God." Psalm 84:2

5. Pain forces us to <u>listen</u> to God.

    "Those who listen to instruction will prosper; those who trust the Lord will be joyful." Proverbs 16:20 NLT

Jesus cares that you are hurting because He is familiar with pain. Remember, He was crucified for our sins. His wrist and feet had six-to-eight-inch nails hammered through them. A crown of thorns was pushed down on His head literally piercing His skull. He endured excruciating pain for several hours as all five liters of blood poured out of His body. Jesus was mocked, rejected, spit upon, and whipped with a cat of nine tails that had steel spikes that ripped the skin off His body. Finally, He had a spear shoved into His side before He died. Jesus knows pain. Jesus understands your pain. Jesus wants to heal your pain.

"Surely he hath borne our griefs, and carried our sorrows: yet we did esteem him stricken, smitten of God, and afflicted. But he was wounded for our transgressions, he was bruised for our iniquities: the chastisement of our peace was upon him; and with his stripes we are healed." Isaiah 53:4-5

Jesus gives us permission to mourn, but now we must give Jesus permission to comfort. Everyone knows the five stages of grief:

1. Denial
2. Anger
3. Bargaining
4. Depression
5. Acceptance

Getting to the point of acceptance when you experience grief is difficult. Only God can truly help you to achieve the level of acceptance you need to be free from your grief. True acceptance means that you embrace the past – both good and bad – and believe that God has a purpose in the pain to help you to help others. God wants to help, so let the Lord begin to heal you starting today.

...FOR THEY SHALL BE COMFORTED.

Summary

Beatitude:

Mourn

Opposing Attitude:

Apathy

God's Reward:

Comfort

How to Develop this Attitude:

"Create in me a clean heart, O God; and renew a right spirit within me.[11] Cast me not away from thy presence; and take not thy holy spirit from me.[12] Restore unto me the joy of thy salvation; and uphold me with thy free spirit.[17] The sacrifices of God are a broken spirit: a broken and a contrite heart, O God, thou wilt not despise." Psalm 51:10-12,17

Chapter 4
BLESSED ARE THE MEEK…

Meekness is definitely a topic that we hear very little about in the world and even in the church. We often avoid subjects that are unfamiliar and uncomfortable within society. So, that is why there is such little understanding about this Fruit of the Spirit that Jesus identified Himself with in Matthew 11:2, *"Take my yoke upon you, and learn of me; for I am meek and lowly in heart: and ye shall find rest unto your souls."*

If Jesus is meek, then we need to understand exactly what meekness is all about, so we can become more like Him. The Merriam-Webster dictionary defines meekness as, "enduring injury with patience and without resentment." I define it as, "humility on steroids." With man, obtaining meekness is impossible, so we need the Lord to help us accept and apply the tough truths of meekness.

Ten Truths of Meekness

1. Meekness is not easily provoked.

   "Be not hasty in thy spirit to be angry: for anger resteth in the bosom of fools." Ecclesiastes 7:9

Everyone seems to want to "provoke the bear" and "ruffle our feathers", but when meekness rules our heart, it becomes more difficult for us to become angry at others' foolish behavior. Meekness controls its feelings and emotions.

2. Meekness is not weakness; it is boldness.

"Now I Paul myself beseech you by the meekness and gentleness of Christ, who in presence am base among you, but being absent am bold toward you:" 2 Corinthians 10:1

Paul was telling us that not only is meekness not weakness, but meekness is boldness. Paul actually taught us that meekness and boldness are not contradictory, but complimentary. Meek people are fearless people, not fearful people. Meekness takes strength.

3. Meekness is God's cure for pride.

"And he said to them all, If any man will come after me, let him deny himself, and take up his cross daily, and follow me. For whosoever will save his life shall lose it: but whosoever will lose his life for my sake, the same shall save it. For what is a man advantaged, if he

gain the whole world, and lose himself, or be cast away?" Luke 9:23-25

Pride is a sin, and meekness is its' cure. In order to fully follow Christ, we must give up our personal right to respond in the flesh when we are attacked and take up the cross and follow Christ. Pride is a disease that only meekness can cure.

4. Meekness is a Fruit of the Spirit.

"But the fruit of the Spirit is love, joy, peace, longsuffering, gentleness, goodness, faith, Meekness, temperance: against such there is no law." Galatians 5:22-23

There are nine fruit of the Spirit that need to be active in our lives if we are claiming that Jesus is our Lord and Savior. The word "fruit" refers to the product or result of something. Apples come from apple trees, and the fruit of the Spirit come from the Holy Spirit when Jesus lives in our hearts. Meekness makes us more like Jesus.

5. Meekness is wisdom in action.

"When pride cometh, then cometh shame: but with the lowly is wisdom." Proverbs 11:2

Walking in wisdom is the key to a successful life. We are never wiser than when we choose to activate our wisdom by putting it into action. If you want to be wise, you have to respond and act in meekness.

6. Meekness unlocks God's power.

"But he giveth more grace. Wherefore he saith, God resisteth the proud, but giveth grace unto the humble." James 4:6

The prideful are an enemy to God. Meekness unlocks the power of God because it proves you are depending on the Lord for help. Meekness is the key to releasing the power of God.

7. Meekness is submission without resistance.

"Submit yourselves therefore to God. Resist the devil, and he will flee from you."
James 4:7

Submission is difficult, but submitting quietly without resisting can only be accomplished with God's help through meekness. The Latin word for meekness is *mansuetude* which means, "to be tamed." We are like wild, untamed animals without meekness.

8. Meekness is about forgiveness.

"And be ye kind one to another, tenderhearted, forgiving one another, even as God for Christ's sake hath forgiven you." Ephesians 4:32

Meekness is grace where we are enabled by the Spirit of God to do what we are unable to do in the flesh. Meekness always offers grace and never seeks justice in the form of punishment for those who offend. Meekness allows you to let the hurts of life slide off your back instead of sticking to your heart. Meekness is not wearing a velcro sweater where everything sticks to it. You will be hurt by the words and actions of others. Meekness is required to have the ability to let it roll off like water off a duck's back, instead of allowing the pain to stick to your heart and negatively affect your future. Forgiveness is more for you than your offender. Meekness is forgiveness.

9. Meekness pursues God's perfect will, not His permissive will.

"Seek ye the Lord, all ye meek of the earth, which have wrought his judgment; seek righteousness, seek meekness: it may be ye

shall be hid in the day of the Lord's anger."
Zephaniah 2:3

When we are meek, we only want what God wants for us. Meekness compels us to never settle for less than God's best in our lives. Meekness always chases after God's perfect will.

10. Meekness admits when it is wrong.

"He that covereth his sins shall not prosper: but whoso confesseth and forsaketh them shall have mercy." Proverbs 28:13

Meek people own up to their mistakes and do not place blame on others. A genuine apology requires strength of character. It shows that you are willing to make things right when you have done wrong. Meekness does not just say, "I am sorry." Meekness says, "I am wrong." Meekness accepts responsibility.

In our current world, people seek power and positions of leadership in order to be in charge. Meekness seems to many like an outdated and antiquated idea. Meekness understands that God promotes and God places people in positions of authority. The promise of meekness in Matthew 5:5 is that we will inherit the earth. Meekness helps us to maintain a modest, moderate, unpretentious, and unassuming life. Meekness does not want the attention or need the spotlight. It does not seek power. Meek people do not have anything to prove. They are not trying to get votes so they can get elected. Meek people do not get elected by men; God appoints them. God's idea of a godly leader, who will one day inherit the authority to rule the earth, revolves around the meaning of meekness. They are strong, submissive, seekers of God's will, understanding, bold, wise, forgiving, humble, courageous, nonviolent, and loving. Wouldn't our world be a better place if our leaders and politicians exhibited those qualities? God wants us to develop the fruit of meekness, so we are ready to inherit the earth and lead the way God wants us to lead.

… FOR THEY SHALL INHERIT THE EARTH.

Summary

Beatitude:

Meekness

Opposing Attitude:

Superiority

God's Reward:

Inherit the Earth

How to Develop this Attitude:

"Take my yoke upon you, and learn of me; for I am meek and lowly in heart: and ye shall find rest unto your souls."
Matthew 11:29

Chapter 5
BLESSED ARE THOSE THAT HUNGER AND THIRST FOR RIGHTEOUSNESS…

Hungering and thirsting for righteousness is about having a passion to fully pursue God, so you can always be in right standing with Him. Passionately pursuing God is the number one desire of God and because of that, His promise is to fill us up when we go after Him.

"But whosoever drinketh of the water that I shall give him shall never thirst; but the water that I shall give him shall be in him a well of water springing up into everlasting life." John 4:14

"And Jesus said unto them, I am the bread of life: he that cometh to me shall never hunger; and he that believeth on me shall never thirst." John 6:35

"In the last day, that great day of the feast, Jesus stood and cried, saying, If any man thirst, let him come unto me, and drink. He that believeth on me, as the scripture hath said, out of his belly shall flow rivers of living water." John 7:37-38

"Ho, every one that thirsteth, come ye to the waters, and he that hath no money; come ye, buy, and eat; yea, come, buy wine and milk without money and without price. Wherefore do ye spend money for that

which is not bread? and your labour for that which satisfieth not? hearken diligently unto me, and eat ye that which is good, and let your soul delight itself in fatness. " Isaiah 55:1-2

"And the Spirit and the bride say, Come. And let him that heareth say, Come. And let him that is athirst come. And whosoever will, let him take the water of life freely. " Revelation 22:17

When you are hungry and thirsty for God you always:

- Want to pray more
- Want to read the Bible more
- Want to give more
- Want to be in church more
- Want to worship more
- Want to serve more
- Want to love more

With physical hunger, you eat and get full. When you are spiritually hungry, you eat and the more you get, the more you want. To understand spiritual hunger and thirst better, it is important to understand the opposite of hungering and thirsting for God is being lukewarm. A lukewarm Christian is when you allow your love for God to fade. It is when things like prayer, reading the Word, and going to church become chores. Being lukewarm and being a

Christian are words that do not go together. It is like saying a "Christian thief" or a "Christian liar".

Smith Wigglesworth was a famous British evangelist in the early 1900's. He believed healing came through faith, and that all his success was due to him being baptized in the Holy Spirit. He once said,

> *"Spiritual hunger is when nothing satisfies us as much as being near to God. Worldliness is that which cools my affection towards God. I'd rather have a man on my platform who is not Spirit-filled, but hungry than a person who is Spirit-filled and satisfied."*

Smith Wigglesworth believed in ministering out of the overflow and not with a heart half full of the Holy Spirit.

God requires us to be zealous and fervent in our pursuit of Him. When we are not sold out, we open ourselves up to misfortune. Ananias in the book of Acts is an example of someone who was lukewarm. He put his love for money and greed before the Gospel. He and his wife, Sapphira, sold their land and gave only a portion of the proceeds to the church, lying about the total amount. This deception was not only sin, but it also revealed their lack of desire to be fully obedient to God. Being lukewarm cost them their lives. The Pharisees, who were religious leaders during Jesus' time, loved power and money. They were more concerned with following their own laws and traditions rather than accepting Jesus as the Messiah. Their prideful and self-righteous attitude caused them to deny the truth and ultimately led to their downfall. Being lukewarm is destructive to our destiny.

Seven Attributes of Lukewarm Christians

1. Lukewarm Christians love with conditions.

    "The Lord hath appeared of old unto me, saying, Yea, I have loved thee with an everlasting love: therefore with loving kindness have I drawn thee." Jeremiah 31:3

    God's love is unconditional and without boundaries. When you are full of God, you are full of love.

2. Lukewarm Christians are double-minded.

    "A double minded man is unstable in all his ways." James 1:8

    Lukewarm people try to figure out how to get the best of both worlds. They never pick sides. They always ride the fence.

3. Lukewarm Christians are content being partially sanitized instead of fully sanctified.

"Whosoever is born of God doth not commit sin; for his seed remaineth in him: and he cannot sin, because he is born of God." 1 John 3:9

Lukewarm Christians do not really want to be saved from their sins as much as they want to be saved from the consequences of their sins.

4. Lukewarm Christians do not have a filter on social media.

"And whatsoever ye do in word or deed, do all in the name of the Lord Jesus, giving thanks to God and the Father by him." Colossians 3:17

People that are half-hearted in their commitment to Christ are not conscious about representing themselves as Christians on social media. They lower their standards and prove their lukewarmness They post photos, videos, gifs, memes, messages, and jokes that will be viewed on Instagram, Facebook, and Twitter that do not glorify God. People are too worried about getting followers. Do not worry about who is following you, but who you are following. Remember, Jesus had only 12 followers! You should be conscientious about your postings and seek to please God instead of man.

5. Lukewarm Christians live by personal preference instead of godly conviction.

"And be not conformed to this world: but be ye transformed by the renewing of your mind, that ye may prove what is that good, and acceptable, and perfect, will of God." Romans 12:2

Preferences can be changed by peer-pressure. Convictions are based on scripture and never change. Lukewarm Christians gauge their "goodness" by comparing themselves to the world. They are satisfied as long as they are not as "bad" as the world.

6. Lukewarm Christians give God their leftovers, not their best.

"Honour the Lord with thy substance, and with the firstfruits of all thine increase:" Proverbs 3:9

When you are sold out to Jesus, you want to give Him your best!!!

7. Lukewarm people are shy or too embarrassed to talk about Jesus or their faith.

"For I am not ashamed of the gospel of Christ: for it is the power of God unto salvation to every one that believeth; to the Jew first, and also to the Greek. For therein is the righteousness of God revealed from faith to faith: as it is written, The just shall live by faith." Romans 1:16-17

Jesus said in the Bible that if you are ashamed of Him on Earth, He will be ashamed of you before God, the Father. When you are really excited about something or someone, you want everyone to know. It is impossible not to want to talk about things you love.

In Revelation 3:14-22, Jesus wrote a letter to the church of Laodicea, condemning them for allowing their fire for God to fizzle and entering into a state of being lukewarm. Jesus told them to be hot or cold, be in or out, yet they became lukewarm, and Jesus declared He would spit them out of His mouth. Jesus hates us being lukewarm. Jesus described being lukewarm to the Laodicea church in five words in Revelation 3:17.

Lukewarm people are:

1. Wretched
   Jesus says when we are lukewarm, we are mentally tormented and physically distressed.

2. Miserable
   Miserable people are extremely unhappy people who do not find any level of comfort.

3. Poor
   Being poor is having a less than adequate supply of something that is desperately needed.

4. Blind
   Lukewarm people may see with their eyes, but they have zero spiritual discernment or judgement. They lack direction and guidance.

5. Naked
   Being spiritually naked is not about having clothes to cover your body. It is about being unarmed and defenseless when you are under attack.

The promise of hungering and thirsting for righteousness, according to Matthew 5, is that we will be filled. God will not abandon or deny anyone who is in full pursuit of being in right standing with

Him. God wants to put as much in you that can be held. The curse of being lukewarm is you will be tormented, unhappy, lacking in every area, have no guidance, and be without the ability to defend yourself when under attack, not to mention that God will want nothing to do with you and even spit you out of His mouth. The only right attitude when it comes to pursuing God is to be fully committed to close any gaps and close any distance by chasing after God, so you will be in right standing with Him. Here is the key to staying on fire for God…Feed your spirit and starve your flesh. Whatever you feed will grow; whatever you starve will die.

…FOR THEY SHALL BE FILLED.

Summary

Beatitude:

Desiring Righteousness

Opposing Attitude:

Independence

God's Reward:

Satisfaction

How to Develop this Attitude:

"And Jesus said unto them, I am the bread of life: he that cometh to me shall never hunger; and he that believeth on me shall never thirst." John 6:35

Chapter 6
BLESSED ARE THE MERCIFUL...

This might be the toughest of the eight attitudes for us as humans to obtain and walk in continuously in our lives. It is impossible to use our fleshly willpower. We must depend on spirit-power to activate mercy. Knowing God means knowing mercy is not just a characteristic that God has, but it is an attribute that defines who God is. God has many characteristics, so we want to make sure that we properly identify each individual one. For instance, grace is not mercy, and mercy is not grace. They are two great but different attributes of God. Grace is getting what we do not deserve. Mercy is not getting what we do deserve. Let me say that again:

Grace = getting what we do not deserve.
Mercy = not getting what we do deserve.

The Old Testament gives us an understanding of exactly what God's mercy involves:

- God is merciful to those who do not deserve it.
- God's mercy accepts our repentance even after a person has continually sinned.
- God eases the punishment of the guilty and does not put people in extreme danger.

- God is slow to anger and patient with both the righteous and the wicked. He gives people time to reflect, improve, and repent instead of punishing sinners immediately.
- God is abundant in kindness to everyone.
- God is compassionate.
- God never goes back on His Word to reward those who serve Him.
- God rewards acts of kindness to everyone.
- God rewards acts of kindness to a thousand generations.
- God forgives willful and intentional sin.
- God forgives and forgets.

The Lord wants us to use His example of expressing mercy as a template to model mercy in our lives towards others. Easier said than done!! Again, with man it is impossible, but with God all things are possible. The promise of showing mercy comes with the reward of receiving mercy in return. That is why this particular attitude is so important for us to demonstrate because however you treat others is, how you will be treated yourself. It is the law of sowing and reaping.

"Be not deceived; God is not mocked: for whatsoever a man soweth, that shall he also reap. For he that soweth to his flesh shall of the flesh reap corruption; but he that soweth to the Spirit shall of the Spirit reap life everlasting. And let us not be

weary in well doing: for in due season we shall reap, if we faint not. " Galatians 6:7-9

The results of your life will be based on the decisions you make, the habits you create, and the promises you break. If I was forced to reduce the complexity of mercy to two words, I would use...

- Compassion
- Forgiveness

Compassion and forgiveness truly describe the nature of God. It truly describes the intent of mercy. It is who and what God is all about. Showing mercy is not just a good suggestion, it is a God-given command. It is required for those who seek to be more like Jesus.

"He hath shewed thee, O man, what is good; and what doth the Lord require of thee, but to do justly, and to love mercy, and to walk humbly with thy God?" Micah 6:8

It is not just having mercy; it is loving mercy.

What Does Mercy Look Like?

1. It is withholding punishment from those who deserve it.
2. It is helping those who have hurt you.

3. It is being kind to those who have offended you.
4. It is being patient with someone who gets on your nerves.
5. It is feeding the hungry and giving drinks to those who thirst.
6. It is clothing the naked.
7. It is giving shelter to the homeless.
8. It is visiting and praying for the sick.
9. It is visiting the prisoners and offering hope.
10. It is accepting an apology from another.
11. It is easing the pain of those who created the pain for themselves.
12. It is slow to get angry when your buttons are being pushed.
13. It is being kind and welcoming to everyone.
14. It is keeping your promises even when it costs you more than you want to pay.
15. It is showing compassion to those who made bad decisions.
16. It gives others time to recover from a loss.
17. It is loving the unlovable.
18. It is seeking grace instead of justice.
19. It is rewarding the good, not seeking revenge for the bad.
20. It is choosing to move on and not allow your past to dictate your future.

Are you still with me? Did you bail to another chapter or close the book altogether? I told you this was not possible to achieve in your flesh no matter how much willpower you use. You need God to help you to actually love mercy. Yes, love it. Showing compassion is not just feeling sorry for people who are suffering. Forgiving others is not saying what someone did to hurt you was "ok" and does not give them permission to continue their bad behavior. Forgiveness is more for you than for your offender. Compassion and forgiveness require premeditation. You have to be prepared to help others and forgive others in advance of a need or offense. So, what can you do to develop mercy in your life?

How to Develop an Attitude of Mercy

1. Repent for having a spirit of apathy.

    "Therefore to him that knoweth to do good, and doeth it not, to him it is sin." James 4:17

    Ask God to forgive you for your lack of concern for others.

2. Read scriptures on mercy.

    "Be ye therefore merciful, as your Father also is merciful." Luke 6:36

    "For he shall have judgment without mercy, that hath shewed no mercy; and mercy rejoiceth against judgment." James 2:13

Reading the Word is the best way to get a revelation from God.

3. Request of God to give you a greater level of love.

    Love solves all problems and heals all wounds.

4. Reflect on how far God has brought you out of darkness.

Be willing to help others as others have helped you.

5. Retire from retirement.

    "But be ye doers of the word, and not hearers only, deceiving your own selves." James 1:22

    Get involved and start practicing mercy until you perfect in it your life.

    Having an attitude of mercy will not always be easy but yield yourself to the Lord so He can give you an anointing to do what is impossible in the natural. No one ever said being like Jesus would be easy, but mercy is required to represent the Lord well here on Earth.

    ...THEY SHALL OBTAIN MERCY.

Summary

Beatitude:

Mercy

Opposing Attitude:

Justice

God's Reward:

Not Getting What is Deserved

How to Develop this Attitude:

"He that covereth his sins shall not prosper: but whoso confesseth and forsaketh them shall have mercy." Proverbs 28:13

Chapter 7
BLESSED ARE THE PURE IN HEART…

Purity is holiness!!! The words "purity" and "holiness" are mentioned throughout the Bible from Genesis to Revelation. "Purity" and "holiness" are also words that are not mentioned much behind the pulpits of America. In many ways, they are offensive words because they create a sense of accountability and a standard that most people in church feel are too high to live up to. However, let us not forget that purity and holiness are attributes that God requires of His people.

"Because it is written, Be ye holy; for I am holy."
1 Peter 1:16

"Speak unto all the congregation of the children of Israel, and say unto them, Ye shall be holy: for I the Lord your God am holy." Leviticus 19:2

So, because God requires us to be pure and holy, it is a topic that must be addressed more. Purity and holiness are attitudes that God desires for all His children to have in their lives. When you are pure, you are free from things that weaken or pollute your soul. Holiness is a big scary word, but when you really understand its basic meaning, it reduces the intimidation of the word. Holy is having our lives yielded.

H = Having
O = Our
L = Lives
Y = Yielded

Purity and holiness are words that have the intent of causing us to make progress in our walk with God every day. Being pure and holy is more about progression than it is perfection. We can only reach a level of purity that God requires when we totally yield ourselves to God. In our full pursuit of God, we should be minimizing the distance between us and the Lord on a daily basis. Our prayer lives should be consumed with selfless, personal requests as much as "what can be removed" and "what can be added" to our lives to draw closer to the Lord.

David has more sins mentioned about him than any other person in the Bible, and he was still considered a man after God's own heart. Why? Because his greatest ability was not to take care of sheep in the fields, play an instrument for a king, lead a nation into victory, or conquer giants in the land. It was his ability to repent and seek the will of God when he did sin.

"Search me, O God, and know my heart: try me, and know my thoughts: And see if there be any wicked way in me, and lead me in the way everlasting."
Psalm 139:23-24

Eight Qualities of Purity and Holiness

1. Pure people are God-conscious.

   "Set your affection on things above, not on things on the earth." Colossians 3:2

   Always keep God on your mind and in your heart to avoid being led astray.

2. Pure people avoid the appearance of evil.

   "Abstain from all appearance of evil."
   1 Thessalonians 5:22

   Pure people do not only have an intention to not engage in sin but to take it to another level and avoid the appearance of sin.

3. Pure people think pure thoughts.

   "Finally, brethren, whatsoever things are true, whatsoever things are honest, whatsoever things are just, whatsoever things are pure, whatsoever things are lovely, whatsoever things are of good report; if there be any virtue, and if there be any praise, think on these things."
   Philippians 4:8

   Our thoughts determine our destiny.

Sow a thought; reap an action.
Sow an action; reap a habit.
Sow a habit; reap a character.
Sow a character; reap a destiny.

4. Pure people are transparent.

"Wherefore putting away lying, speak every man truth with his neighbour: for we are members one of another." Ephesians 4:25

They have nothing to hide. They are an open book.

5. Pure people bear the fruit of the Spirit.

"But the fruit of the Spirit is love, joy, peace, longsuffering, gentleness, goodness, faith, meekness, temperance: against such there is no law." Galatians 5:22-23

The more the fruit of the Spirit grow in your life, the more it will produce a greater level of purity in your life.

6. Pure people separate themselves from evil.

"And ye shall be holy unto me: for I the Lord am holy, and have severed you from other

people, that ye should be mine." Leviticus 20:26

Do not put yourself in a place where temptation can overtake you.

7. Pure people fear God.

"The fear of the Lord is to hate evil: pride, and arrogancy, and the evil way, and the froward mouth, do I hate." Proverbs 8:13

A fear of God is a respect for God. Fearing the Lord does not just mean you are scared of the consequences of sin, it means you love God enough to not want to hurt Him by sinning.

8. Pure people have divine encounters with God.

"In the year that king Uzziah died I saw also the Lord sitting upon a throne, high and lifted up, and his train filled the temple. [2]Above it stood the seraphims: each one had six wings; with twain he covered his face, and with twain he covered his feet, and with twain he did fly. [3]And one cried unto another, and said, Holy, holy, holy, is the Lord of hosts: the whole earth is full of his glory. [4]And the posts of the door moved at the voice of him that

God trusts pure people enough for Him to reveal His power and glory to them.

The reward of purity is seeing God. Most people would say that Jesus is talking about Heaven. I believe that as well; however, I also believe the pure of heart will see the power of God on Earth. The flipside is that the consequence of impurity is that you will not see God or inherit the Kingdom of God. The scriptures are noticeably clear concerning the specific sins you need to refrain from in order to avoid missing out on spending eternity with Christ. The following two scriptures give us a good start at sins we need to avoid.

Know ye not that the unrighteous shall not inherit the kingdom of God? Be not deceived: neither fornicators, nor idolaters, nor adulterers, nor effeminate, nor abusers of themselves with mankind, Nor thieves, nor covetous, nor drunkards, nor revilers, nor extortioners, shall inherit the kingdom of God. And such were some of you: but ye are washed, but ye are sanctified, but ye are justified in the name of the Lord Jesus, and by the Spirit of our God." 1 Corinthians 6:9-11

"Now the works of the flesh are manifest, which are these; Adultery, fornication, uncleanness, lasciviousness, Idolatry, witchcraft, hatred, variance, emulations, wrath, strife, seditions, heresies, Envyings, murders, drunkenness, revellings, and such like: of the which I tell you before, as I have also told you in time past, that they which do such things shall not inherit the kingdom of God." Galatians 5:19-21

Sins to Avoid to Remain Pure and Holy

- Adultery
- Fornication
- Hatred
- Greed
- Stealing
- Strife
- Divisions
- Stealing
- Lying

- Anger
- All sexual immorality

Being pure and holy is all about separating yourself unto God and fully yielding to His will. God would never ask you to be pure if it were not possible to attain in your life. Here is the key…seek God, not purity!!! Purity will only manifest itself in your life when you pursue God in your life.

"But seek ye first the kingdom of God, and his righteousness; and all these things shall be added unto you." Matthew 6:33

…FOR THEY SHALL SEE GOD.

Summary

Beatitude:

Pure in Heart

Opposing Attitude:

Deception

God's Reward:

See God

How to Develop this Attitude:

"Mortify therefore your members which are upon the earth; fornication, uncleanness, inordinate affection, evil concupiscence, and covetousness, which is idolatry:" Colossians 3:5

Chapter 8
BLESSED ARE THE PEACEMAKERS…

In a world that has never been more divided, there is a need for peacemakers like never before. Peacemakers are committed to minimizing conflict and maximizing peace. According to scripture, a peacemaker is not just someone who wants peace, but a peacemaker is one who is actively trying to reconcile people to God and to one another.

There Are Two Kinds of People

1. Troublemakers
2. Peacemakers

I have heard messages preached on peace but never on being a peacemaker, but if there is chaos in the world, then we ought to be peacemakers in the world. There are differences in the world and in the church, so we need peacemakers to mediate reconciliation. A peacemaker is a person who helps solve a conflict and reach a peaceful solution between parties who disagree, quarrel, or fight. If two countries are engaged in war, peacemakers help negotiate a truce. Gandhi was known for being a peacemaker. Moms often must be peacemakers when their children have disputes. At times, pastors have to broker peace between parishioners in their churches. In other words, there are times when we all have interceded on someone's behalf and acted as a peacemaker. We should all seek peace, and we should all desire to be peacemakers. So, let us answer two important questions:

1. What is peace?
2. What is a peacemaker?

What is Peace?

The definition of peace is simple: it is freedom from disturbance. It is tranquility. Peace is quiet amid noise. The opposite of peace is fear, worry, and anxiety. Spiritually speaking, there are two kinds of peace:

1. Peace with God

> *"And the work of righteousness shall be peace; and the effect of righteousness quietness and assurance for ever."*
> Isaiah 32:17

> Peace with God comes at salvation when you confess your sins and accept Jesus as your savior. Peace with God is knowing you are not at war with God, and you are on His side.

2. Peace of God

"And the peace of God, which passeth all understanding, shall keep your hearts and minds through Christ Jesus." Philippians 4:7

The peace of God is what we need to get through this thing called life. The Peace of God comforts you in times of distress and discouragement.

We all need peace in a world of confusion and trouble. To have peace in the middle of trouble, we need a peace with God and the peace of God from the God of peace.

Six Interesting Facts Concerning Peace

1. Sometimes you have to go to war in order to obtain peace.
2. Peace is a fruit of the Spirit, so the more Holy Spirit you get, the more peace you will have.
3. Peace is not the absence of difficulties; it is the calmness God gives in the midst of trouble.
4. Peace is the umpire to help us discern if things should be "safe" or "out" in our lives.
5. One of Jesus' names is the Prince of Peace.
6. The peace of God gives us a longer lasting life.

Having a peace of God and a peace with God is finding a place of spiritual harmony with God and mental wholeness in your mind. The peace that God gives supersedes all of Earth's negative circumstances.

What is a Peacemaker?

1. A peacemaker is a mediator.

   They engage in bringing people or parties together to engage in constructive discussions that lead to mutually agreeable solutions. The difference between a mediator and an arbitrator is that a mediator manages the process, and an arbitrator makes a decision.

2. A peacemaker is impartial.

   Peacemakers never take the side of individuals; they always take the side of "what is right", not "who is right."

3. A peacemaker is a negotiator.

   Peace does not come at just one person's expense. Negotiation is about compromise and finding solutions that create a win-win situation for everyone.

4. A peacemaker is peaceful.

Peacemakers cannot create peace among others if they do not first start with peace in their own hearts. How are we to calm tempers or reconcile with another if we are not at peace in our own lives? We do not need hostile peacemakers.

5. A peacemaker is patient.

Peacemaking is tough, hard, messy, and dirty work. In trying to work things out, it might get worse before it gets better. It often takes more time to reconcile things than what we want, so patience is necessary. You must willingly tolerate a lot without getting frustrated to ultimately reach a conclusion.

6. A peacemaker is wise.

It takes wisdom from God's Word to provide solutions that create peace. Wisdom is an instrument used to reach peace with parties who are fighting.

7. A peacemaker is a risk-taker.

Peacemaking is risky because you put yourself in a hazardous situation when you are in the middle of two parties that are disagreeing. There is always a risk of losing or not accomplishing your goal of peace.

8. A peacemaker is a listener.

Peacemakers listen carefully and validate the feelings of others. Listening is the key to beginning to end any conflict. It is important to validate people's feelings because feelings are real. However, feelings can also overpower logical solutions. Peacemakers help to keep the balance between addressing feelings and creating the best solution for everyone.

9. A peacemaker uses the Word of God to help decide matters.

The Bible is a great tool that God wants us to use in order to achieve peace. All the answers and all the solutions of life can be found in the Word of God. Here are some good scriptures to keep in mind when it comes to peace.

"Now the God of hope fill you with all joy and peace in believing, that ye may abound in hope, through the power of the Holy Ghost." Romans 15:13

"Great peace have they which love thy law: and nothing shall offend them."
Psalm 119:165

"Let him eschew evil, and do good; let him seek peace, and ensue it." 1 Peter 3:11

"For God is not the author of confusion, but of peace, as in all churches of the saints."
1 Corinthians 14:33

"When a man's ways please the Lord, he maketh even his enemies to be at peace with him." Proverbs 16:7

"Glory to God in the highest, and on earth peace, good will toward men." Luke 2:14

"For the kingdom of God is not meat and drink; but righteousness, and peace, and joy in the Holy Ghost." Romans 14:17

10. A peacemaker is active and not passive.

Peacemakers take the initiative to get involved to bring healing and reconciliation.

A Peacemaker has Three Jobs

1. Discern the Problem
2. Disarm the Parties
3. Discuss the Prescription

A peacemaker's job is not easy. It is definitely a calling that comes from God. The true children of God only have that title when they are at peace with God and are looking to be peacemakers of God. Peace and peacemaking are attitudes that we must demonstrate in our lives as children of God.

…THEY SHALL BE CALLED THE CHILDREN OF GOD.

Summary

Beatitude:

Peacemaker

Opposing Attitude:

Troublemaker

God's Reward:

Called Children of God

How to Develop this Attitude:

"Be of the same mind one toward another. Mind not high things, but condescend to men of low estate. Be not wise in your own conceits. [17] Recompense to no man evil for evil. Provide things honest in the sight of all men.[18] If it be possible, as much as lieth in you, live peaceably with all men.[19] Dearly beloved, avenge not yourselves, but rather give place unto wrath: for it is written, Vengeance is mine; I will repay, saith the Lord." Romans 12:16-19

Chapter 9
BLESSED ARE THEY WHICH ARE PERSECUTED FOR RIGHTEOUSNESS' SAKE…

Here is the last of the eight attitudes that Jesus encourages us to have in our lives. This is an attitude where no matter what someone says to you, or how much persecution you may face, you respond in a proper manner. The words "persecuted" and "reviled" in Matthew 5:11 are about verbal abuse. It is about being harassed by people who will call you names or say other cruel words because they do not like your spiritual stance or your religious beliefs that are based on scripture.

What is Persecution?

- Harassment
- Being Annoyed
- Unfair Treatment
- Being Threatened
- Being Abused
- Being Hated
- Imprisonment
- Death

When Muslims are attacked, we call it Islamophobia.
When Jews are attacked, we call it Antisemitism.
When Christians are attacked, we call it Persecution.

According to Open Doors and For the Martyrs organizations...

- China attacked, damaged, or destroyed or closed over 5,000 churches in 2022.
- Nigeria martyred over 1300 Christians in 2022.
- North Korea has been ranked the most dangerous place for Christians, 20 years in a row.
- One out of seven Christians have experienced severe persecution.
- Fifty-nine percent of Christians in America say they experienced some level of persecution.

Since 1999, lifewayresearch.com records that there have been approximately twenty-four different fatal church shootings in the USA:

- 1999 - Wedgewood Baptist Church in Fort Worth, Texas
- 2001 - Greater Oak Missionary Baptist Church in Hopkinsville, Kentucky
- 2002 - Our Lady of Peace Catholic Church in Lynbrook, New York
- 2003 - Turner Monumental AME Church in Kirkwood, Georgia
- 2005 - Living Church of God in Brookfield, Wisconsin
- 2005 - World Changers Church in College Park, Georgia

- 2006 - Zion Hope Missionary Baptist in Detroit, Michigan
- 2006 - Ministry of Jesus Christ Church in Baton Rouge, Louisiana
- 2007 - First Presbyterian Church in Moscow, Idaho
- 2007 - First Congregational Church in Neosho, Missouri
- 2007 - New Life Church in Colorado Springs, Colorado
- 2008 - First Baptist Church in Maryville, Illinois
- 2009 - Reformation Lutheran Church in Wichita, Kansas
- 2012 - World Changers Church in College Park, Georgia
- 2015 - Emanuel AME Church in Charleston, South Carolina
- 2017 - Burnette Chapel Church of Christ in Antioch, Tennessee
- 2017 - First Baptist Church in Sutherland Springs, Texas
- 2017 - St. Alphonsus Church in Fresno, California
- 2019 - West Freeway Church of Christ in White Settlement, Texas
- 2022 - The Church in Sacramento in Sacramento, California
- 2022 - Geneva Presbyterian Church in Laguna Woods, California

- 2022 - Cornerstone Church in Ames, Iowa
- 2022 - St. Stephen's Episcopal Church in Vestavia Hills, Alabama
- 2024 – Lakewood Church in Houston, Texas

What we have now that Jesus did not deal with then is computers and social media. Unnamed people can sit behind a desk and type whatever they want to damage someone's reputation. They have "computer courage." They put things on the internet they would never say to your face. In part. that is why many Christians think silence is golden and they refuse to speak up and speak out for Christ. It is also why we have so many weak-kneed, limp-wristed, wimpy preachers in the pulpit who preach a non-offensive, politically correct message that "pets devils" instead of "casting out devils." We are officially the 2 Timothy 3:5 generation, *"Having a form of godliness, but denying the power thereof: from such turn away."*

We have a form of godliness, we have mastered the art of religion, and we have become nothing more than professional Christians. However, we have no power or anointing to destroy yokes and remove burdens. The Bible tells us to turn away from those who are playing games with God and just going through the motions. It is time we get serious about serving God. It is time to get back to speaking up about righteousness instead of hiding in our closets and being too scared to speak out because someone may hurt our feelings with their words. Serving God does not always mean blessings; sometimes it involves suffering. That is a part of Christianity we do not want to talk about.

Eight Facts About Persecution

1. All that will live godly will suffer persecution.

    "Yea, and all that will live godly in Christ Jesus shall suffer persecution." 2 Timothy 3:12

    Notice that it says… ALL. All, not some, but everyone who will or chooses to be godly, will suffer persecution. Godly in Greek means "to be devoted."

2. Love your enemies and pray for those who persecute you.

    "But I say unto you, Love your enemies, bless them that curse you, do good to them that hate you, and pray for them which despitefully use you, and persecute you;" Matthew 5:44

    This verse tells us to love your enemies and pray for those who persecute you. It is hard to hate someone and respond inappropriately when you are praying for them.

3. You are in good company when they persecute you.

"Remember what I told you: 'A servant is not greater than his master.' If they persecuted me, they will persecute you also. If they obeyed my teaching, they will obey yours also." John 15:20

Martyrs in the Bible

- John the Baptist was beheaded.
- Onesiphorus and Porphyrios were tied to wild horses and dragged to death.
- Mark was dragged to death.
- Stephen was stoned to death.
- Andrew was crucified.
- Peter was crucified upside down.
- Priscilla and Aquila were killed.
- Bartholomew was tortured and beheaded.
- Phillip was stoned to death.
- Barnabas was burned alive.
- Thomas was tortured and burned in a furnace.
- James, the brother of Jesus, was beaten to death.
- Matthew was beheaded.
- Matthias was stoned and beheaded.

- Luke was hung.
- Timothy was stoned to death.
- Jesus was crucified.

A martyr is someone who dies for Christ. A true Christian is someone who lives for Christ. It is a lot harder to live for Christ than it is to die for Him. They talked badly about Jesus. They are going to talk badly about you.

4. It is only a blessing to be persecuted for your righteous beliefs, not your unrighteous actions.

"Blessed are they which are persecuted for righteousness' sake: for theirs is the kingdom of heaven. Blessed are ye, when men shall revile you, and persecute you, and shall say all manner of evil against you falsely, for my sake." Matthew 5:10-11

You do not get some free pass from verbal slander when you are living a hypocritical lifestyle. Count it an honor to suffer or be ridiculed for standing up for Christ.

5. Persecution is not strange.

"Beloved, think it not strange concerning the fiery trial which is to try you, as though some

strange thing happened unto you:" 1 Peter 4:12

Expect persecution whenever you do the right thing. Do not be surprised when others attack your spiritual beliefs.

6. Persecution has a godly purpose.

"But the God of all grace, who hath called us unto his eternal glory by Christ Jesus, after that ye have suffered a while, make you perfect, stablish, strengthen, settle you."
1 Peter 5:10

This scripture tells us that suffering has four purposes.

Four-Fold Purpose for Pain

1. Perfects you
2. Stablishes you
3. Strengthens you
4. Settles you

7. Let God deal with those who persecute you.

"Dearly beloved, avenge not yourselves, but rather give place unto wrath: for it is written, Vengeance is mine; I will repay, saith the Lord." Romans 12:19

"Vengeance is mine," says the Lord!

8. Persecution makes the hot Christians hotter, and the cold Christians colder.

   "And great fear came upon all the church, and upon as many as heard these things."
   Acts 5:11

   Do not let persecution keep you from God, let it draw you closer to Him.

Why Do We Rejoice When We Are Persecuted?

1. Because your rejoicing is a sound of victory that the enemy hates.

   If God loves something and the devil hates it, then I am all in. It messes with the devil when we are supposed to be down because of his attacks, and yet we rejoice instead.

2. Because your rewards come in Heaven.

   Heavenly rewards that come from God are way better than earthly rewards that come from man.

3. Because you are on the right track.

The greatest of prophets suffered for living righteous lives. You can be counted among the best that have ever lived when others speak against you.

The things God asks of His children are not easy. That is why it takes strength to be a Christian in the days we live in. All the attitudes are tough, and this one may be one of the most difficult to manifest. However, obedience to this attitude is the kingdom of Heaven. All our suffering on Earth cannot compare to the rewards God has for us in Heaven. Everything that Heaven offers is ours when we walk in obedience to God's Word!!! The question is, "Will you live for Christ?", not just "Will you die for Christ?" Death is sometimes easier than obedience. Be willing to live for Christ through the persecution. You have to remind yourself that as you suffer for Christ, you will also reign with Him.

… FOR THEIRS IS THE KINGDOM OF
HEAVEN.

Summary

Beatitude:

Rejoice when persecuted!

Opposing Attitude:

Bitterness

God's Reward:

Inherit the Kingdom of Heaven

How to Develop this Attitude:

"Beloved, think it not strange concerning the fiery trial which is to try you, as though some strange thing happened unto you:[13] But rejoice, inasmuch as ye are partakers of Christ's sufferings; that, when his glory shall be revealed, ye may be glad also with exceeding joy.[14] If ye be reproached for the name of Christ, happy are ye; for the spirit of glory and of God resteth upon you: on their part he is evil spoken of, but on your part he is glorified." 1 Peter 4:12-14

Conclusion

Jesus' first message may have been one of His most important. He understood the importance of attitudes because how we feel affects how we act. The Lord wants us to represent Him as ambassadors and have a kingdom attitude at all times.

What is a Kingdom Attitude?

1. Be Humble
2. Be Tender-hearted
3. Be Meek
4. Be Passionate
5. Be Merciful
6. Be Pure
7. Be Peacemakers
8. Be Strong in Persecution

These eight attitudes are kingdom attitudes. These attitudes reflect how we can represent and honor the Lord on the earth in order to build the kingdom of God. The devil wants to ruin our reputation by causing our flesh to rise up and respond in a way that does not glorify God. This life is a constant battle between the flesh and the spirit.

"Watch and pray, that ye enter not into temptation: the spirit indeed is willing, but the flesh is weak."
Matthew 26:41

The way to win the battle is to stay closely connected to the Lord and walk in obedience to the scriptures. Having a godly attitude not only pleases God, but it confirms to the world that we are a new creation in Christ. A godly attitude is a positive attitude that offers encouragement in a depressing world. A godly attitude is a loving attitude that shows the love of God in a hateful and divided world. A godly attitude is a faithful attitude that reflects faithfulness in everything you do in life. We were not born with a good attitude, so we have to learn to have a good attitude. In our learning, let us remember that our outward conduct is determined by our inward character. If things are right in our hearts, things will be good everywhere else in our lives. Let us get our hearts right and then keep our hearts right. The Beatitudes or attitudes that "ought to be" are a great place to start in getting things going in the right direction. There are eight Beatitudes and the number eight in the Bible reflects a new beginning. Allow God to begin something new in your life by applying these truths to your life today. These Beatitudes help us look at life through the lens of God. God wants to open our eyes. When God releases a revelation, He wants us to:

- Look Around
  Look around you and realize where you are at is your mission field and you are the missionary.

- Look Down

  Look for those God will put in your life who need a hand-up, not a handout.

- Look Up

  Keep your eyes on Jesus, so through your actions and behavior others will be drawn to the Lord.

- Look Out

  Open your eyes to see those who need to experience the love of God.

- Look Forward

  Put the past behind you, and look forward to the amazing things God will release in your life when your attitude aligns with His.

Let the revelation of this book open your eyes to the expectations God has for you and the blessings that come when we walk in obedience to His commands. Have a good, godly attitude that reflects your commitment to Christ. Let the fruit of the Spirit that you are inwardly developing become the attitudes you reflect outwardly.

Overview of the Beatitudes

Beatitude	Oppoisng Attitude	God's Reward	How to Develop This Attitude
Poor In Spirit	Pride	Kingdom of Heaven	James 4:7-10
Mourn	Apathy	Comfort	Psalm 51
Meekness	Superiority	Inherit the Earth	Matthew 11:29
Desiring Righteousness	Independence	Satisfaction	John 6:35
Mercy	Justice	Not Getting What is Deserved	Proverbs 28:13
Pure in Heart	Deception	See God	Colossians 3:5
Peacemaker	Troublemaker	Called Children of God	Romans 12:16-19
Rejoice when Persecuted	Bitterness	Inherit the Kingdom of Heaven	1 Peter 4:12-14

82

To get daily wisdom nuggets, check out Pastor Bill on social media for the most important minute of your day!

The Minute That Matters

Scan the QR code with your phone, and you will be automatically connected to your choice of social media.